I, Matthew Henson

POLAR EXPLORER

CAROLE BOSTON WEATHERFORD

illustrated by ERIC VELASQUEZ

BLOOMSBURY
CHILDREN'S BOOKS
NEW YORK LONDON OXFORD NEW DELHI SYDNEY

BLOOMSBURY CHILDREN'S BOOKS
Bloomsbury Publishing Inc., part of Bloomsbury Publishing Plc
1385 Broadway, New York, NY 10018

BLOOMSBURY, BLOOMSBURY CHILDREN'S BOOKS, and the Diana logo are trademarks of
Bloomsbury Publishing Plc

First published in the United States of America in January 2008 by Bloomsbury Children's Books
Paperback edition published in January 2022

Bloomsbury books may be purchased for business or promotional use. For information on bulk purchases
please contact Macmillan Corporate and Premium Sales Department at specialmarkets@macmillan.com

ISBN 978-1-5476-0896-6 (paperback)

The Library of Congress has cataloged the hardcover edition as follows:
Weatheford, Carole Boston.
I, Matthew Henson / Carole Boston Weatherford ; illustrations by Eric Velasquez.
p.   cm.
ISBN-13: 978-0-8027-9688-2 • ISBN-10: 0-8027-9688-5 (hardcover)
ISBN-13: 978-0-8027-9689-9 • ISBN-10: 0-8027-9689-3 (hardcover)
1. Henson, Matthew Alexander, 1866–1955—Juvenile literature. 2. African-American explorers—
Biography—Juvenile literature. 3. North Pole—Discovering and exploration—Juvenile literature.
I. Velasquez, Eric, ill. II. Title.
G635.H4W43   2008   910.911'3—dc22   2007020144

Art created with Prismacolor Nupastel and Prismacolor Soft Pastel on Wallis Paper
Typeset in Minister Bold
Printed in China by C&C Offset Printing Co., Ltd., Shenzhen, Guangdong
10 9 8 7 6 5 4 3 2 1

To find out more about our authors and books visit www.bloomsbury.com
and sign up for our newsletters.

To my mother, Carolyn Boston, who steered me toward the horizon.
To Ron, who always believed I'd reach the goal.
To Caresse and Jeffery, who witnessed my journey.
—C. B. W.

Crossing that bridge with lessons I've learned . . . (SEAL)
—E. V.

I did not walk forty miles
from the nation's capital
to Baltimore's busy harbor to eye
ships from a dock. Though just thirteen,
I yearned for a taste of the adventures
that I had heard old sailors speak of,
to explore the seven seas
and somehow find my calling.

I did not start as cabin boy, climb
the ranks to able-bodied seaman,
sail to five continents, and learn
trades and foreign tongues to be shunned
by white crews who thought Blacks
were not seaworthy. I did not chart
this course to drift in humdrum jobs
ashore. My dreams had sails.

I did not take a job as a stock boy
at a men's store to work my way up
the ladder to clerk. I yearned for wind
at my back. So when a customer,
a naval officer, said he needed
a manservant for an expedition
to Nicaragua to map a canal,
I signed on without a second thought.

I did not sail to the tropics just to launder shirts and cook meals. I meant to prove myself as an explorer. That chance came when the chainman fell ill and I joined the survey crew. In the swampy jungle, I learned Peary as well as I knew the ropes. And he leaned on me like his right-hand man.

I had not earned Peary's trust to part ways and turn my back on adventure. *Next trip,* he said, *you'll have to work like three men.* On the *Kite* with five others, we sailed to Greenland. I alone learned to speak Inuktut, and built our base camp while Peary charted a journey to the North Pole. To go *there*, I would work like a horse.

I did not befriend the Inuit, learn
to build a sledge, handle a dog team,
track and hunt on ice, and kill a polar bear
to let an Inuit legend freeze me with fear.
*Kokoyah, the Devil of the North, guards
the ice cap*, the Inuit warned. But their story
did not scare me. After they danced and drummed,
I played the accordion and sang hymns.

I did not sail north with Peary again and again
through the frozen sea, charting
the ice cap, inching toward the Pole,
where no man had stood,
for frostbite to halt our mission.
When ice took most of Peary's toes,
I carried him back alive—Kokoyah
on our heels, howling in the wind.

We had not braved the frozen wilderness,
going miles beyond the last village,
only to starve because new snow
hid our store of food. We tracked
hare and musk ox until the hunting
was poor and we were skin and bones.
Then, we ate our dog team—all
but one. Kokoyah churned in our guts.

We had not survived the frigid cold
that broke some and killed others
to let our dream melt when hope
and cash ran low. While others gave up,
we returned to the polar region
and, guided by the Inuit, fetched
a prize from the ice cap—a meteor,
which Peary sold to raise funds.

I did not explore the Arctic to sit still between voyages while Peary planned. I became a railroad porter and explored my own land. In the South, I met hate face-to-face. And in New York, I met Lucy, who loved me though I didn't have a cent. I promised her the Pole as a wedding gift. Before we could marry, I had to set sail.

WHITE ONLY !

Peary and I had not sailed the *Roosevelt*,
a new ship built to cut through icy seas,
only to set out on foot from our base camp
and have our path blocked by melted ice.
But turn back we did, tricked by Kokoyah again.
Back home, we both knew our next trip
would be our last. I now had a wife,
and we were no longer young men.

Peary had not handpicked seven men—
and timed our trip so I had the six-month winter night
to build sledges, train dog handlers, and enlist
Inuit guides—for our last try to fail.
In the long daylight of spring, two dozen men
and 130 dogs struck out like teams in a relay,
pushing across the ice to store food and supplies
for the team that would go farther.

We had not faced sudden storms, frozen peaks
and ridges, and shifting iceberg castles
to let leads, patches of open water, swallow us.
With a quarter ton of supplies and an often-injured
Peary on a sledge, we crossed twenty miles in
as many hours. Snow pricking our faces, fingers
burning with cold, we built igloos each night
and dared Kokoyah to stop us.

I had not stuck by Peary for two decades,
sharing the same goal, only to reach a fork
when our journey was on its last leg.
Tasks completed, team after relay team
returned to base camp. In the end,
Peary picked me to go all the way, vowing
he could not make it without me.
Kokoyah would be no match for us.

We had not trudged on, rushing across
the ice pack with four Inuit,
to let faulty instruments steer us wrong.
I used dead reckoning to guide us north.
Sluggish from the cold, Peary sent me ahead.
Miles later, I stopped the sledge,
wiped my frozen lashes, and scanned
the vast sheet of ice. I was close.

Shortly, Peary arrived and we broke through
the thin ice. He did a sounding, lowered
nine thousand feet of rope into the ocean. Six men—
one Black, one white, four Inuit—had reached
the North Pole. *We have found what we hunted*,
I said in Inuktut. A camera froze our feat in time.
But we had not come for photos; we came
to plant our flag. And Kokoyah was nowhere in sight.

Author's Note

In 1866 Matthew Henson was born to sharecropper parents in Nanjemoy, Maryland. In 1867 his family moved to Washington, D.C., to escape racism and poverty. As a boy, he heard a speech by Frederick Douglass, the most famous African American leader of the time. Douglass's words inspired Matthew to dream of becoming great. By 1879 Matthew had lost both his parents, dropped out of school, and left home. He walked from Washington to Baltimore, where he found work in a restaurant. There, he listened to an old sailor's tales of the sea.

Seeking adventure, thirteen-year-old Matthew signed on as cabin boy with the *Katie Hines*. He sailed to five continents, studying literature, mathematics, and navigation with Captain Childs. But after the captain died, Matthew could not find another ship whose crew would treat him as an equal.

Disillusioned, he was working as a stock boy in a men's store when a chance meeting with a customer, naval officer Robert Peary, changed the course of his life. Peary aimed to be the first man to stand on the North Pole—a goal Henson readily shared. Driven by a love of exploration, the two men, along with small teams of explorers, made seven trips to the Arctic region from 1891 to 1909. Twice on the polar ice cap, Henson saved Peary's life. But neither danger nor lack of funds deterred them. On April 6, 1909, Peary and Henson stood together at the Pole—making history.

But back home, controversy greeted the two explorers. Dr. Frederick A. Cook, who had accompanied Peary and Henson on an earlier trip, falsely claimed to have reached the Pole in 1908. Some authorities dismissed Peary's achievement because a Black man had accompanied him. Henson gave lectures to prove that Peary was telling the truth. However, Peary responded by downplaying Henson's role in the expedition. By the time their record-breaking feat was acknowledged, Peary and Henson had parted ways. Admiral Peary died in 1920.

In the years that followed, Henson, who retired from a job as a messenger for the U.S. Custom Service in 1936, was honored by the Explorers Club in New York, Howard University, the Geographic Society of Chicago, the U.S. Congress, the U.S. Navy, Dillard University, and President Dwight D. Eisenhower. Matthew Henson died in 1955. Finally, in 1988 Henson was moved to Arlington National Cemetery to be buried beside Peary. In 2000 Henson was recognized with the National Geographic Society's Hubbard Medal for distinction in exploration, discovery, and research.